D1365270

GREEK MYTHS

PANDORA'S VASE

A RETELLING BY
CARI MEISTER

ILLUSTRATED BY
McLEAN KENDREE

PICTURE WINDOW BOOKS
a capstone imprint

CAST OF CHARACTERS

TITANS (TY-TENZ): gods who ruled the world before the Olympians conquered them

ZEUS (ZOOS): son of Rhea and Cronus; Olympian god of sky and ruler of mankind

OLYMPIANS (OH-LIHM-pi-enz): gods led by Zeus who ruled from Mount Olympus

PROMETHEUS (PROH-MEE-thee-UHS): brother to Epimetheus; Titan who brought fire to man

EPIMETHEUS (EP-uh-MEE-thee-UHS): brother to Prometheus; Titan married to Pandora

HEPHAESTUS (HUH-FES-tuhs): son of Zeus; god of fire who made Pandora

APHRODITE (AF-RUH-DY-TEE): goddess of love

ATHENA (AH-THEE-NUH): goddess of wisdom and skill

APOLLO (UH-POL-OH): god of the sun, music, and healing

HERMES (HUR-MEEZ): messenger of the gods and the god of travelers

PANDORA (PAN-DOHR-UH): wife of Epimetheus; first woman, designed by Zeus, made by Hephaestus

WORDS TO KNOW

MERCHANT—a person who sells something

MOUNT OLYMPUS—the home of the Olympian gods

MYTH—a make-believe story that seems to be true

NYMPH—a female spirit of the natural world

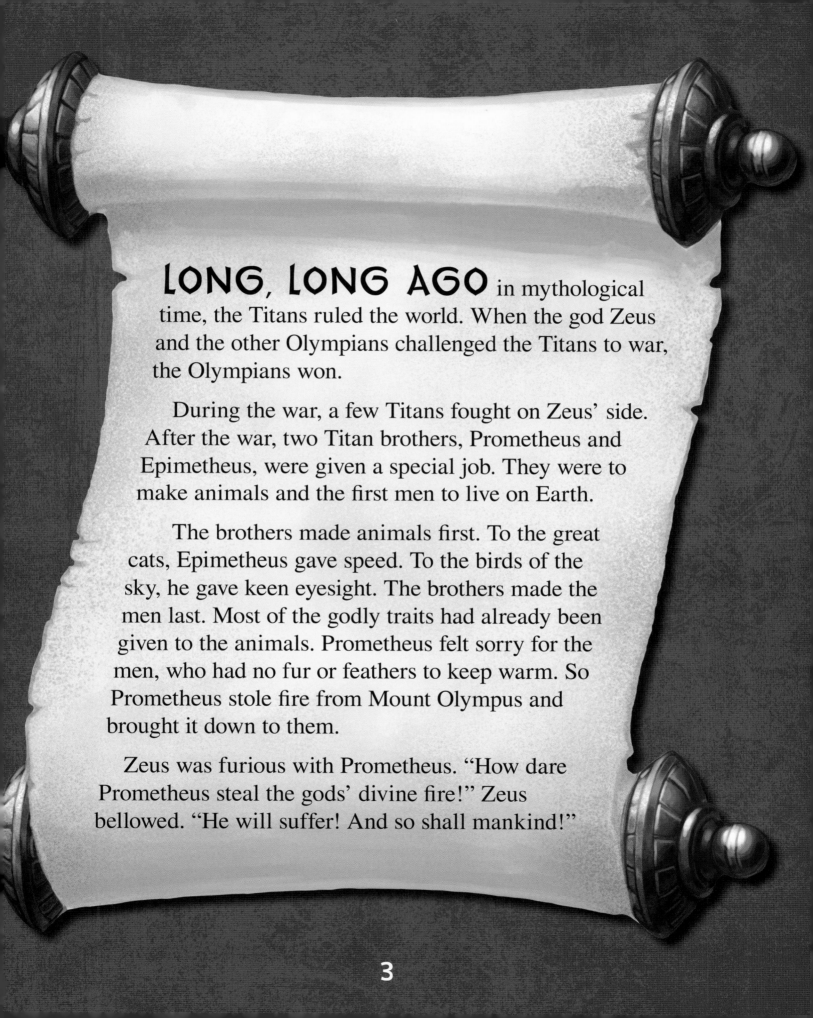

LONG, LONG AGO in mythological time, the Titans ruled the world. When the god Zeus and the other Olympians challenged the Titans to war, the Olympians won.

During the war, a few Titans fought on Zeus' side. After the war, two Titan brothers, Prometheus and Epimetheus, were given a special job. They were to make animals and the first men to live on Earth.

The brothers made animals first. To the great cats, Epimetheus gave speed. To the birds of the sky, he gave keen eyesight. The brothers made the men last. Most of the godly traits had already been given to the animals. Prometheus felt sorry for the men, who had no fur or feathers to keep warm. So Prometheus stole fire from Mount Olympus and brought it down to them.

Zeus was furious with Prometheus. "How dare Prometheus steal the gods' divine fire!" Zeus bellowed. "He will suffer! And so shall mankind!"

Zeus' punishment to Prometheus was swift and severe. Zeus commanded his son Hephaestus to bind Prometheus and leave him tied to a rock. There, day after day, a great bird would peck away at his liver.

Zeus was even more clever in his punishment for man. He asked Hephaestus to create the first woman. She would be Epimetheus' partner. And she would be a tool to bring about man's downfall.

"She must be so beautiful that Epimetheus will be unable to resist her," Zeus said.

Hephaestus used Aphrodite, the most beautiful god, as his model for the woman.

Zeus commanded the gods to give the woman special gifts.

The goddess Athena made an elegant gown and an embroidered veil. She also taught the woman skills such as weaving and needlepoint.

Apollo gave the woman the gift of music.

Hermes gave her the gift of speech and persuasion. But he also gave her a cunning nature and, above all, curiosity. He named the woman Pandora, meaning "all gifts."

Zeus examined Pandora. "Yes," he said, "she is ready. She is beautiful and gifted. Epimetheus will be unable to resist her. Hermes, take Pandora down to Earth. Tell Epimetheus she is a gift from me."

Hermes carried Pandora down to Earth and presented her to Epimetheus.

Everyone who saw Pandora was dazzled. She mesmerized them.

When Epimetheus stared into Pandora's eyes, he smiled. "I accept this gift from Zeus," he said.

Just as Zeus had hoped, Epimetheus and Pandora soon were married.

Shortly after Pandora and Epimetheus were married, a large package arrived at their home.

"A gift from Zeus," said the messenger. "Make sure you read the card."

Pandora could not resist tearing open the wrapping. She gasped when she saw the gift. "It's beautiful!" she cried.

There, in front of her, was a vase—but not just any vase. It was a golden vase with elaborate carvings. Pandora's fingers traced around birds, horses, and nymphs.

Epimetheus was surprised by Zeus' grand gift. He opened the card. As Epimetheus read it, Pandora's hand reached to the top of the vase.

"Wait!" screamed Epimetheus as he grabbed his wife's hand. "Don't open the lid!"

"Why not?" she asked.

"Zeus has commanded it!" he said. Epimetheus looked at his wife. She was staring at the vase.

"Pandora," he said, "we must never open this vase!"

Pandora looked at her husband.

"Never!" he repeated.

She ran out the door and down to the river.

ENJOY THE BEAUTY OF THE VASE. ENJOY THE WAY THE GOLD SHINES IN THE SUNLIGHT. ENJOY THE STORIES OF THE CARVINGS. BUT NEVER, EVER OPEN THE LID.

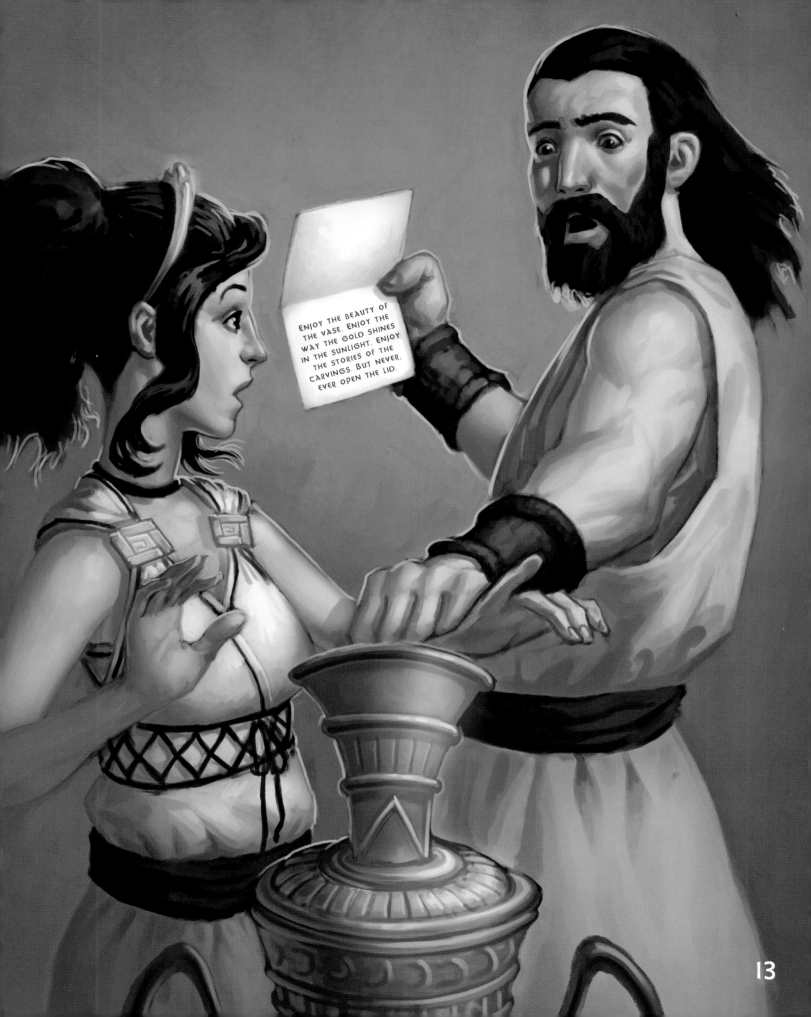

"Never open the lid?" Pandora cried. "How is that possible?"

Pandora looked at her reflection in the river. Her tears blurred her vision. She wiped them on her gown.

A wood nymph heard her cries and helped her dry her tears.

"Zeus has commanded that I never open the golden vase," said Pandora, "but I'm just so curious."

The nymph felt sorry for Pandora. She tried to keep Pandora's mind occupied by changing the colors of the flowers.

Pandora sat by the flowers for a while, but her mind kept returning to the vase.

"Perhaps," she said, "I should go to the market and open vases. Then I will not feel the strong desire to open the golden vase."

Pandora ran back to the stable and saddled up her horse. In a few minutes she was on the worn path that led to the marketplace. It was not long before she found the vase merchant.

The vases were lined up in rows—from smallest to tallest.

Pandora's heart fell as she saw how dull they were in comparison to her golden vase at home.

"But," she thought, "it might help."

Pandora ran her fingers over some of the vases. "Do you mind if I open them?" she asked the merchant.

"Please do," said the merchant.

Pandora started with the smallest vase. It wasn't much bigger than her hand. She opened each vase, peering into the bottom. When she finished opening the largest one, she sighed with disappointment.

"Do any of them please you, my lady?" asked the merchant.

"Oh, they are all well made and of good quality," Pandora said. "But they are not quite what I was looking for."

"I do have one more," said the merchant.

The merchant went to the back of the stall and pulled out a small package.

"I found this on my travels east," he said.

Pandora's heart leaped. Perhaps *this* would stop her curiosity about the vase at home.

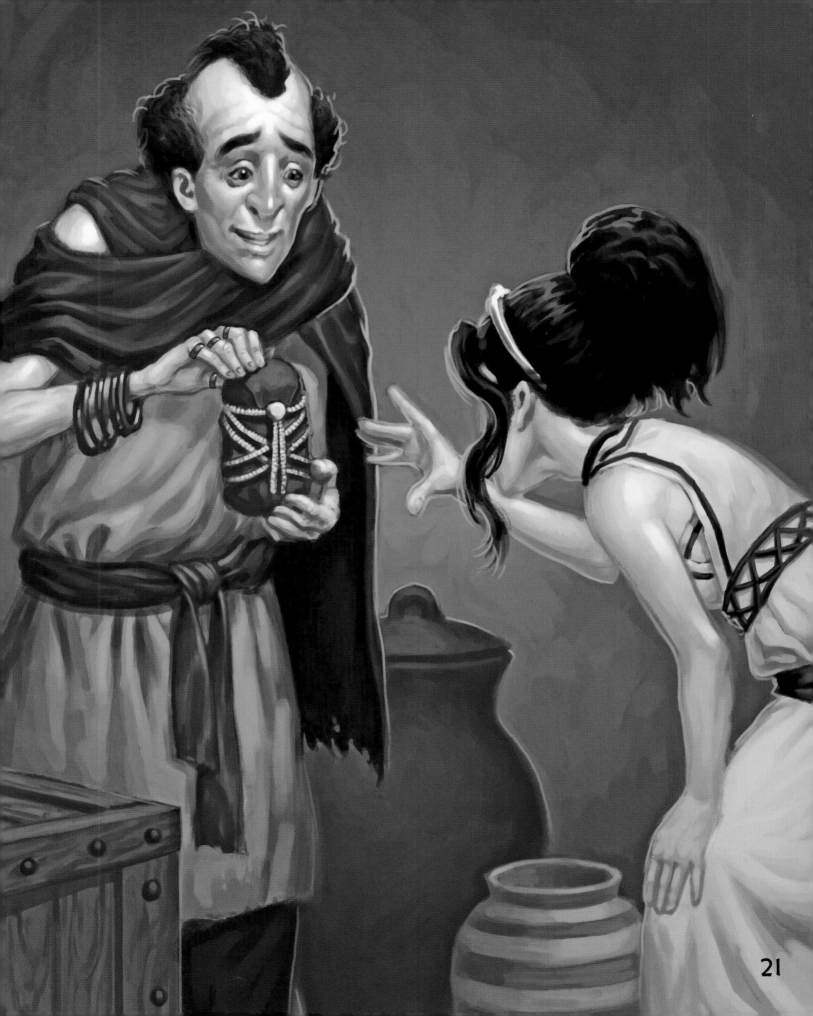

Carefully, Pandora opened the package. Inside was a lovely bronze vase with golden swirls. She opened the top. There was an enticing smell—a little sweet, but with a hint of something woodsy and faraway.

"It's very nice," she said to the merchant as she handed him a silver coin. "Thank you."

Pandora slipped the little vase into her pocket and rode home. She lingered in the stable for as long as she could.

"I must go in and show Epimetheus my little vase," she finally said.

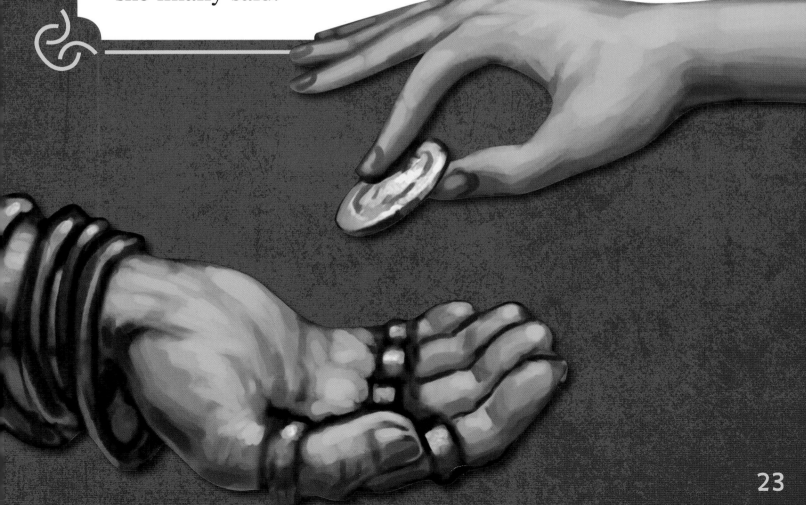

When Pandora walked through the door, she gasped. The sun was streaming in through the windows, making the vase shine brightly.

"It's so beautiful!" she said.

Pandora stared at the vase for a long time. She ran her fingers around the carvings. "I can't stand it!" she said. "I must open it!"

Her heart sped up. She glanced around quickly. She was alone. Surely one little peek wouldn't upset the gods.

Pandora touched the lid. The gold felt warm and cool at the same time. Her heart pounded. Her hands started to sweat. She couldn't wait any longer!

And then Pandora lifted the lid.

A gust of wind burst violently from the vase, pushing Pandora to the floor.

RAGE

GREED

WAR

JEALOUSY

DESPAIR

PANIC

Pandora watched in horror as the evils of mankind flew out of the vase and circled above her.

Pandora struggled to get up from the floor. But she was too late—all of the evils had escaped.

With shaking hands, Pandora finally replaced the lid. She was terrified. But then she realized that something was still in the vase. **Hope** remained.

At the thought of hope, Pandora felt relief. She hugged the vase tightly.

Just as Zeus had planned, Pandora had released the evils. Mankind would suffer forever.

But Pandora had also discovered hope. And **hope** always remains.

I AM HOPE.

READ MORE

Daly, Kathleen N., and revised by Marian Rengel. *Greek and Roman Mythology, A to Z*. New York: Chelsea House Publishers, 2009.

Namm, Diane. *Greek Myths: Retold from the Classic Originals*. Classic Starts. New York: Sterling, 2011.

Saunders, Nick. *Pandora's Box*. Graphic Greek Myths and Legends. Milwaukee: World Almanac Library, 2007.

INTERNET SITES

FactHound offers a safe, fun way to find Internet sites related to this book. All of the sites on FactHound have been researched by our staff.

Here's all you do:

Visit *www.facthound.com*

Type in this code: 9781404866683

 Check out projects, games and lots more at
www.capstonekids.com

LOOK FOR ALL THE BOOKS IN THE GREEK MYTHS SERIES:

THE BATTLE OF THE OLYMPIANS AND THE TITANS

JASON AND THE ARGONAUTS

MEDUSA'S STONY STARE

ODYSSEUS AND THE CYCLOPS

PANDORA'S VASE

THE WOODEN HORSE OF TROY

Thanks to our adviser for his expertise and advice:
Terry Flaherty, PhD
Professor of English
Minnesota State University, Mankato

Editor: Shelly Lyons
Designer: Alison Thiele
Art Director: Nathan Gassman
Production Specialist: Sarah Bennett
The illustrations in this book were created digitally.

Picture Window Books
151 Good Counsel Drive
P.O. Box 669
Mankato, MN 56002-0669
877-845-8392
www.capstonepub.com

 All books published by Picture Window Books are manufactured with paper containing at least 10 percent post-consumer waste.

Library of Congress Cataloging-in-Publication Data
Meister, Cari.
 Pandora's vase : a retelling / by Cari Meister; illustrated by McLean Kendree.
    p. cm. — (Greek myths)
 Includes index.
 ISBN 978-1-4048-6668-3 (library binding)
 1. Pandora (Greek mythology)—Juvenile literature. I. Title.
 BL820.P23.M45 2012
 398.20938'02—dc22   2011006986

Printed in the United States of America in North Mankato, Minnesota.
032011   006110CGF11